Presented to

_____

by _____

on _____

PRAYERS
for little hearts

Illustrated by Elena Kucharik

Tyndale House Publishers, Inc.
CAROL STREAM, ILLINOIS

Visit Tyndale's exciting Web site for kids at www.tyndale.com/kids.

TYNDALE is a registered trademark of Tyndale House Publishers, Inc.
Tyndale Kids logo is a trademark of Tyndale House Publishers, Inc.

Little Blessings is a registered trademark of Tyndale House Publishers, Inc.
The Little Blessings characters are a trademark of Elena Kucharik.

Prayers for Little Hearts

Prayers by James C. Galvin of The Livingstone Corporation. The prayers in this book
are based on the text of *The Simplified Living Bible,* copyright © 1990 by KNT Charitable Trust.
All rights reserved.

Designed by Catherine Bergstrom

The verses quoted in the introduction of this book are taken from the *Holy Bible,*
New International Version,® NIV.® Copyright © 1973, 1978, 1984 by Biblica, Inc.™
Used by permission of Zondervan. All rights reserved worldwide.

For manufacturing information regarding this product, please call 1-800-323-9400.

Library of Congress Cataloging-in-Publication Data

Prayers for little hearts / illustrated by Elena Kucharik.
     p. cm.
   Summary: A collection of prayers based directly on verses from the Bible and
intended for young children.
   ISBN 978-0-8423-4970-3
   1. Children–Prayer-books and devotions–English 2. Prayer. [1. Prayer books
and devotions. 2. Prayers.] I. Kucharik, Elena, ill. II. Tyndale House Publishers.
BV265.P73 1996
242'.82–dc20   95-40114

Printed in Mexico

12 11 10
18 17 16 15 14

Prayer is a gift from God. God wants parents to pray for their children and with their children. He wants us to teach our children to pray. But when are children ready to learn about prayer? A simple guideline for parents is that as soon as children are able to talk, they are ready to pray. Certainly a child cannot grasp all that prayer means or everything that it does for us. But they can understand that prayer is simply talking to their heavenly Father.

God wants children to come to him in prayer:

> *When Jesus saw this, he was indignant. He said to them, "Let the little children come to me, and do not hinder them, for the kingdom of God belongs to such as these." (Mark 10:14)*

God wants children to call him their heavenly Father:

This, then, is how you should pray: "Our Father in heaven, hallowed be your name." (Matthew 6:9)

God wants children to make requests to him:

For everyone who asks receives; he who seeks finds; and to him who knocks, the door will be opened. (Matthew 7:8)

God wants children to pray about any need:

Do not be anxious about anything, but in everything, by prayer and petition, with thanksgiving, present your requests to God. (Philippians 4:6)

God wants children to pray every day:

Be joyful in hope, patient in affliction, faithful in prayer. (Romans 12:12)

God wants children to pray at any time of the day:

> Be joyful always; pray continually; give thanks in all
> circumstances, for this is God's will for you in Christ
> Jesus. (1 Thessalonians 5:16-18)

God wants all of his children to praise him:

> Praise our God, all you his servants, you who
> fear him, both small and great! (Revelation 19:5)

All of the following prayers are based directly on
verses from the Bible. Together with your child, you
can look up the reference included with each
prayer. It's never too early for little children to learn
to pray. It's never too late for parents to start
teaching their children to pray.

Dear God,

Please help me to love

you with all my heart and

with all my soul and with all

my strength.

In Jesus' name, Amen.

from Deuteronomy 6:5

Dear God,

You are very loving and
kind. You always keep your
promises. Please help me to
do my best for you.
In Jesus' name, Amen.

from I Kings 8:23

Dear God,

You are very powerful.

Everything in heaven and

on earth is yours. Help me

want to obey you.

In Jesus' name, Amen.

from I Chronicles 29:11

Dear God,

I want to pray to you

every day. Help me to pray

with all my heart.

In Jesus' name, Amen.

from Psalm 5:3

Dear God,

Help me to praise you

with all my heart. I want

to tell everyone about the

great things you do.

In Jesus' name, Amen.

from Psalm 9:1

Dear God,

I love you so much!

You have done so many

great things for me.

In Jesus' name, Amen.

from Psalm 18:1

Dear God,

Keep me from doing wrong

things on purpose. I want

my words and thoughts to

always please you.

In Jesus' name, Amen.

from Psalm 19:13-14

Dear God,

Create in me a new, clean
heart. Please fill my heart
with clean thoughts and
right desires.
In Jesus' name, Amen.

from Psalm 51:10

Dear God,

When I am afraid,

I will trust in you.

In Jesus' name, Amen.

from Psalm 56:3

Dear God,

You give me strength.

I will sing your praises

because you are my

place of safety.

In Jesus' name, Amen.

from Psalm 59:9

Dear God,

I will call to you when

trouble happens. Thank you

for being there to help.

In Jesus' name, Amen.

from Psalm 86:7

Dear God,

You made all the parts of

my body. Thank you for

making me so wonderfully!

In Jesus' name, Amen.

from Psalm 139:13-14

Dear God,

No one else is like you.

You are great, and your

name is full of power.

In Jesus' name, Amen.

from Jeremiah 10:6

Dear God,

I don't want to hide your

light! Let my good deeds

glow for all to see.

In Jesus' name, Amen.

from Matthew 5:15-16

Dear God,

Please help me to treat

others the way I would

like them to treat me.

In Jesus' name, Amen.

from Matthew 7:12

Dear God,

Thank you for forgiving

my sins. Please help me to

forgive other people, too.

In Jesus' name, Amen.

from Mark 11:25

Dear God,

Oh, how I praise you!

I rejoice in God my Savior!

In Jesus' name, Amen.

from Luke 1:46-47

Dear God,

Thank you for sending

Jesus to die so that we

can have eternal life.

In Jesus' name, Amen.

from John 3:16

Dear God,

Help me to love others just

as much as you love me.

In Jesus' name, Amen.

from John 13:34

Dear God,

Please help me not to get

tired of doing right. Help

me not to give up.

In Jesus' name, Amen.

from Galatians 6:9

Dear God,

Show me how to honor my

father and mother. Please

help me to obey them.

In Jesus' name, Amen.

from Ephesians 6:1-2

Dear God,

Please help me to stay

away from complaining

and arguing.

In Jesus' name, Amen.

from Philippians 2:14

Dear God,

Help me not to worry

about anything but to pray

about everything.

In Jesus' name, Amen.

from Philippians 4:6

Dear God,

Help me to trust you for

the problems I face each

day. Help me to grow

closer to you.

In Jesus' name, Amen.

from Colossians 2:6

Dear God,

Help me to always be

joyful. Help me to always

keep on praying.

In Jesus' name, Amen.

from I Thessalonians 5:16-17

Dear God,

Thank you that we can

ask you for wisdom. Please

give me a lot of it.

In Jesus' name, Amen.

from James 1:5

Dear God,

Please help me to be a good

listener. Help me not to

become angry with others.

In Jesus' name, Amen.

from James 1:19

Dear God,

Help me to learn more

and more about Jesus.

In Jesus' name, Amen.

from 2 Peter 3:18

Dear God,

Help me to really love

people. Help me to prove

it with my actions.

In Jesus' name, Amen.

from I John 3:18

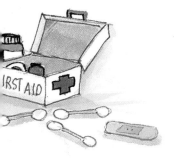

Dear God Almighty,

You are worthy to receive

glory and honor and power.

You have created all things.

In Jesus' name, Amen.

from Revelation 4:11

Prayers for Special Days

With everything else parents have to do to prepare for special occasions, we can miss the opportunity to help point out God's blessings in our children's lives. In the Old Testament God directed the nation of Israel to build an altar or offer a sacrifice on special occasions. Today God is pleased when his people honor him with prayers of thanks for the special events in their lives. Praying with our children on their special days helps them understand that all good things come from God. Here are some prayers for special days.

Dear God,

Thank you for letting me
be born. Thank you for
giving me life. Thank you
for another birthday. Help
me to live for you.
In Jesus' name, Amen.

Dear God,

Thank you for all the presents that people give us at Christmas. And thank you for giving Jesus to us as the best gift of all.

In Jesus' name, Amen.

Dear God,

I'm sad that Jesus died on
the cross to pay for sin.
But I'm glad that he paid
for my sin. Thank you for
raising him to life again!
In Jesus' name, Amen.

THANKSGIVING

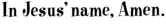

Dear God,

Thank you for giving me
food, clothes, and a place
to live. Thank you for my
family and relatives. Please
help me to be more thankful
on other days, too.
In Jesus' name, Amen.

MOTHER'S DAY

Dear God,

Thank you for my mom.

Please give her a good day.

Please help me to love and

obey her all the time.

In Jesus' name, Amen.

FATHER'S DAY

Dear God,

Thank you for my dad.

Please give him a good day.

Please help me to love and

obey him all the time.

In Jesus' name, Amen.

GRANDPARENTS' DAY

Dear God,

Thank you for Grandma and

Grandpa. They are special

to me. Thank you that I am

special to them, too. Please

take care of them.

In Jesus' name, Amen.

Dear God,

Thank you for my new school. Help me not to be afraid. Please help my teacher to help me learn and grow.

In Jesus' name, Amen.

MAKING FRIENDS

Dear God,

Thank you that I got to

meet a new friend today.

Help me to be a good friend.

Thank you for being a

friend to us.

In Jesus' name, Amen.

TAKING A TRIP

Dear God,

Thank you that we get

to go on this fun trip.

Please keep us safe as we

travel. Help us to get

along as a family.

In Jesus' name, Amen.

Books in the Little Blessings line

- *Prayers for Little Hearts*
- *Questions from Little Hearts*
- *What Is God Like?*
- *Who Is Jesus?*
- *What about Heaven?*
- *Are Angels Real?*
- *What Is Prayer?*
- *Is God Always with Me?*
- *Why Is There a Cross?*
- *What Is the Bible?*
- *Who Made the World?*

- *The One Year Devotions for Preschoolers*
- *The One Year Devotions for Preschoolers 2* (available soon)
- *God Loves You*
- *Thank You, God!*
- *Many-Colored Blessings*
- *Blessings Come in Shapes*

- *God Created Me!* A memory book of baby's first year

CP0216